The Modern Manifesto

When I was a young boy, we were all taught about American history through a lens of mythical reverence. Washington crossing the Delaware, Abraham Lincoln fighting for freedom and freeing the slaves, stories of good vs evil. When we elected our little student council members, the most popular, charismatic kid would win. These views and habits were ingrained in us. We still view political leaders as the sorts of people you want to build a statue of; we are fooled by charisma and charm and often seem to forget that governing is an actual serious job, not a symbolic role.

With a questionable economy, increased criminal and political violence, dangerous conspiracies, and a new Cold War emerging, our need for competent government has arguably never been greater. We are engaged in a great test of character, examining whether this nation can continue to thrive or whether it is beginning its long predicted decline in the vein of Rome, Persia, and the other great empires of world history.

This manifesto is based on a simple premise: America has lost its way. Reasonable voices who champion responsible governance, civil discourse, and compromise are drowned out by incessant theatrics and loud, radical voices. Even those who may otherwise be stoic civil servants can be pulled along with the current. We are left with an endless tug of war between competing ideologies and the normal function of government is inhibited. It is time for the metaphorical adults here to grab this thing by the scruff of the neck and make everyone knock off the crap. Americans by and large just want to live our lives freely, be treated fairly, and feel secure. Unfortunately, politics seems to always get in the way of the work the government should be doing.

In the following pages, I will lay out a case for returning aspects of government to their constitutional roots and voluntarily changing the ways we view and interact with politics. The goal here is to highlight some of the areas in which American politics have gone the most off course. By educating ourselves on the way government works, the way it was intended to work, and what other influences are at play, we can allow ourselves to treat politics in a more stoic and practical manner, leading to better efficiency, better representation, and more satisfaction with the direction of our country and our communities.

Part 1

1. Fixing Our Expectations and View of Government

The last three American presidents have all been elected as symbols. Hope and change, the brash outsider, rejecting Trumpism. It is rather silly that the fate of our entire country hinges on marketing slogans and personality cults. And this is not just about who ends up winning presidential elections. Hillary Clinton was a symbol of equality for women in her second place campaign, for example.

Nor is it just about who competes in presidential elections. The good people in a House district in Georgia elect Marjorie Taylor Greene as their representative, even though she more or less focuses 100% of her time in the media over national level culture war issues and 0% of her time representing the specific interests of her district or seriously legislating. Why? Because she is an ideological symbol.

There is a prevailing expectation for whomever we elect to proudly carry the flag of our chosen ideology and fiercely battle the political enemies who seek to forge our country into a hellscape modeled on their own deranged ideology. The problem, of course, is that the person you choose to carry the sword is not a hero in a fantasy novel. They are not going to single handedly slice through partisan gridlock, implement everything they intend, and create the utopia we envision. And that's OK.

We do not need every president to be George Washington nobly crossing the Delaware. We do not need, and do not want, every Congressperson to be a radical partisan who refuses to compromise. We think that way because we expect our side to win all the time and we fail to see the legitimate concerns of our neighbors. But it is well past time to recognize the reality of politics on this scale.

In the words of the great Rolling Stones, you can't always get what you want. But if you try sometime, you'll find you get what you need. Donald Trump, Barack Obama, Bernie Sanders, and AOC are not superheroes. They are human beings. They are flawed. They are limited. And they probably do not agree with you on everything anyway. The work of government is not the work of a single man with a single plan. It requires input from a number of different areas, consultation with experts, and the dirty C word: COMPROMISE.

It should be abundantly clear that the expectation for our side to run the entire country by decree is flawed. Expecting political dominance is always going to end in disappointment, especially to those on the farther ends of the political spectrum. And refusing to compromise with our neighbors means they will refuse to compromise with us.

We need to recalibrate our expectations of elected officials. We need to tell them that responsible governance is more important than Twitter. We need to reward them for compromising to get things done and punish them when they are ideological stumps who only want to obstruct.People want to cast all kinds of aspersions and blame on elected officials and media, which is definitely fair to an extent. But it is utterly deranged to conveniently excise our own role from the discussions. We, the electorate, choose who occupies those positions. Media responds to our consumption habits. Any change must start on the ground level with us, We The People.

And thus I am challenging you to question the way you vote, the way you interact with political topics, the ways in which you develop your beliefs and ideals and priorities. What good does it do to flip between Republican and Democratic governments while accomplishing nothing that either side wants? Are you looking for gratification, pride, and other personal emotions? Or are you looking for practical, positive changes? Are you looking to confirm your beliefs? Or are you seeking objective truth? Do you want somebody to lead the government in a mundane but responsible manner or an ideologue personality cult?

We need to change our perspective on government and adjust our expectations accordingly. We need to make government about governing responsibly again.

Who would make a better leader: an extreme partisan who revels in political games and shady fundraising and backroom dealing or a level-headed, stoic intellectual who just wants to do his job well? If we do not attach a party or ideology to it, I suspect nearly all you would say the latter. But what would happen if I attached ideology? What if it was an ardent socialist or a classical liberal or a nationalist? What if it magically changed to read whatever ideology or party you most identify with?

How far would you let this person go in pursuing your joint political desires? What if they wanted to suppress votes or overturn fair elections in the name of the supposed greater good? What if they want to amend the constitution to take out term limits and future elections and just hold power? How many of you would go along with it? If you say you wouldn't, how many people do you know that would?

A bit alarming to consider, isn't it? The good news is that we can fix American governance with the steps laid out here. But it starts with us. It starts in our own homes with our own habits.

There has never been a better time to change course. Our last two presidents will both be in their 80s in the 2024 election cycle. Congressional leadership is being challenged on both sides of the aisle. We can force change now. Support responsible candidates who are not mere mouthpieces for their party or ideology. Support transparency and fair reporting. Support decorum and civility, reject personal attacks and symbolism.

Instead of looking for who can bring the most radical changes, look for who can run the show. You are the ones who are going to change things. All you need to start is a hard worker and deal maker who will work on your behalf.

2. Fixing the Presidency

The legislative branch makes laws, the executive branch executes them. This was the basic separation of powers we were taught in elementary school. But over the course of American history, this has become less true over time and may never have been as farcical as it is today.

Politics are more nationalized than ever and all of that power culminates in the president. But this was not always the case and certainly was not the intent of the founders. The core constitutional duties of the president are to manage the executive branch, command the military, and lead diplomacy.

Our focus on a president's legislative agenda betrays the original intent of the job. The president's contemporary focus on legislation comes from two sources: one formal (but misused) and one informal.

Formally, the president has power to veto legislation. But this was not intended to be used as a sword to force the legislature into passing the president's agenda. It was meant as a shield-- a check on absurd bills and constitutional encroachment-- and this is how it was used in the early days of the republic.

The first six presidents issued a grand total of eight formal vetoes and two pocket vetoes. No recent president has finished their service in the single digits. Even the ones who served only a single single term. The role of the veto has clearly expanded significantly from its original use. The Federalists Paper 73 speaks of the veto preventing "depredation" by a legislature which could otherwise strip much of the executive's power. It speaks of the veto in terms of self-defense for the executive branch and the constitution. Here is one excerpt on the "case for which it is chiefly designed:"

"In the case for which it is chiefly designed, that of an immediate attack upon the constitutional rights of the Executive, or in a case in which the public good was evidently and palpably sacrificed, a man of tolerable firmness would avail himself of his constitutional means of defense."

It was not designed to strong-arm a legislative agenda.

Informally, the president takes a lot of legislative authority simply by being the biggest draw in his party. This very notion turns representative democracy on its head.

The house is supposed to be representative of localized areas of the country and speak and vote specifically on their behalf. But the whole thing is now completely nationalized. Policy objectives come from the top down. The president has an agenda and Congress better fall in line or else they'll get primaried by supporters of the president, which harms their reelection prospects. If they're in his party, of course. If they're not, they have to outright reject everything he says for the same reasons.

But isn't that backwards? Shouldn't House members bring problems and solutions from their districts? Shouldn't senators be telling the president what their states need instead of the other way around?

Perhaps we should just generally expect the president to sign the bills congress passes unless they raise some significant non-partisan issue as envisioned in Federalist 73. And what have recent presidents even accomplished, anyway?

Donald Trump's biggest legislative goals were to repeal and replace the Affordable Care Act and to "build the wall," a wall on the southern border "from sea to shining sea" that Mexico would pay for. He nickel and dimed some small parts of a wall without the legislature and Mexico did not pay for it. He did not repeal the Affordable Care Act and never had a plan to replace it.

Barack Obama's most significant bill was the Affordable Care Act, which both sides of the aisle already want to replace. It has already been gutted in a number of ways and it will almost certainly be replaced before it is 20 years old.

George W. Bush was supposed to be the education president, but No Child Left Behind is universally panned. The most consequential legislation from his presidency are the Patriot Act and the authorizations to use military force. Disasters across the board.

It's really, really hard to get significant bills passed. And even when they get it through, it tends to fall short of expectations. Yet all anyone talks about (of substance, anyway) during the campaigns is the competing legislative agendas. We should know better by now.

Despite popular belief, the president does not control the economy. In virtually every case of a good or bad economy, the forces outside the president's control are much stronger than the forces in it. For example, could President Donald Trump have done more to save the economy when COVID struck? He could have done some things differently, but it's unlikely it would have made so significant an impact as to save the economy at that time. The global economy took a dump and COVID was spreading everywhere. Even the modern president only has so many powers in his own country, let alone the rest of the globe.

President Bill Clinton's booming 90s economy was always going to happen. The dot-com boom. It would have happened under any president. Perhaps NAFTA helped some, perhaps other tweaks and ripple effects helped and hurt some. But the dot-com boom was always going to be the major economic driver at that time.

Even congressional gridlock can largely be laid at the feet of our current treatment of presidents. The real bad partisan obstruction of which Senator Mitch McConnell, Speaker Nancy Pelosi, et al. subscribe really revolves around the presidency. It's largely about making the other party's president look bad so that your party can win the next one.

Congressional elections follow trends prompted by presidential elections. For example, you can count on an incumbent president's party losing congressional seats in the midterm. The best way for congressional Republicans to do well is to make President Biden look bad. And vice versa with Democrats and President Trump before and same with President Obama and Republicans and so on.

In the constitution, it is clear that the primary role of the president is that of a non-partisan professional. He is the commander in chief of the armed forces. He is the head of diplomacy. He is the leader of the executive branch. These are the primary functions of the presidency under Article II. The supposition at the time of Washington was that a president would put politics to the side and treat the job as a sober professional. This seems like a silly thought today, but only because we have tolerated the opposite for so long.

Electing a president based on the core constitutional areas of diplomacy, military, and management of the executive branch, plus allowing Congress the freedom to legislate without depending on the president would be better than the all or nothing, extreme ideological swings we see in the federal government every few years. It narrows the criteria we have to evaluate and allows the president to focus on the core areas of his job rather than balancing complex domestic and international policy considerations.

Despite these ideological swings, gridlock persists on big ticket items and the biggest promises from each president. If we shift our focus, we can judge presidents on simple and relatively clear criteria.

Military, diplomacy, and executive management.

3. Elect Congress To Represent and Legislate

The House of Representatives is where elected Representatives from small districts all over the country meet to implement federal policy that (in theory) benefits their constituents. It is a federal job passing federal laws.

The idea is that besides having their views on national politics represented, the elected Representative actually tries to get specific benefits for their district. Abortion, military budget, etc. are only a small portion of the job. A good representative looks to subsidize the industries his or her constituents rely on. He or she tries to get federal contracts in her district. That can be frustrating when turned up to 11 as pork barrel spending and is often seen as negative, but it is important to have an advocate for your community in Congress. The key is to keep the decision making objective.

Someone like Marjorie Taylor Greene does none of those things for her community. She focuses on her brand of national politics. Hell, she isn't even serving on any committees and has expressed pleasure at this fact because it means she has more time to be an internet troll.

Because she does not do any committee work or address local issues or participate in any meaningful work, the people in Representative Greene's district are getting less representation than their fair share. They are not getting full representation in Congress. This is not meant as an attack on Representative Greene, it is simply a fact: Nobody is advocating for the particular needs of this district. And perhaps worst of all, they largely don't even understand that she is supposed to be doing these things.

Representative Greene and others see politics only in terms of sides and teams and opposition. They would gladly sacrifice the ordinary work of Congress in order to get more famous and demonstrate fealty to their side. They often interrupt official state business to make political theater and they never compromise or do anything productive whatsoever. It should go without saying that Congress is not an appropriate forum for using performative politics to score culture war political points. It is a real, serious job. But yet, here we are.

Confirmations of posts the President assigns are becoming more theatrical and more detached from their original purposes every election cycle. Merrick Garland should be on the Supreme Court. Brett Kavanaugh's confirmation did not need to become such a circus. Ketanji Brown Jackson's confirmation was hijacked by Ted Cruz ranting about critical race theory and specific children's books about race. And these are just the highly publicized confirmations. Opposition parties in Congress try to tie up routine appointments these days. Ambassadors, other federal judge positions, everything the president appoints. This is because the people we send to Congress are so obsessed with their own power, media exposure, and party/ideology that they would sacrifice the very function of the republic in order to keep a federal judge spot open until their side wins an election. It is insane and clearly counterproductive.

Additionally, Congress must be allowed latitude to legislate without being under a president's thumb or gridlocking along partisan lines. As the makers of law under the constitution, Congress is supposed to use their collective judgment to legislate what is needed to move the country forward. But that judgment needs to be based on more than R or D in order to be truly effective.

As voters, we can change how we choose and evaluate legislators. We can reward cooperation. Cooperation does not mean giving in. A good negotiator can give up something less meaningful to him in order to acquire something more meaningful. Allowing legislators to hide behind party instructions is the easy way out. Force them to think for themselves and put in the work.

We can reward legislators who spend more time working and less time fundraising. We can reward the ones who work things out for the best rather than the ones who halt the whole process out of fear of being seen as collaborators with the enemy. We can choose legislators who do not see the other party as the enemy. We can choose to elect smart, capable, hard-workers and keep performers on Twitter and YouTube where they belong.

We can vote out legislators like Greene who do not put in the work or the Democrats who insist on punishing their colleagues for breaches of decorum. Don't get me wrong, we should expect a level of decorum and respect among colleagues in our government, but we do not necessarily need to make it official government business.

We can vote out ideologues and obstructionists and those merely seeking to use Congress to make money or advance their careers. Some people we do elect will end up as those things anyway, yes, but then we can vote them out. We do not have to elect incumbents ad infinitum. The power is in our hands.

Perhaps the biggest shame here is that we merely choose not to exercise the power we are given and mindlessly vote R or D or incumbent or challenger without regard for more particulars. I am challenging you to challenge yourself and your Congressional candidates. Look into all of the candidates in your primaries and general elections. I would bet that you like one who isn't the front runner, perhaps even one who does not align with your normal party.

"But my vote will not matter if I do not vote for one of the top candidates." To that I say, how much does your vote count anyway? Out of millions of possible choices, you end up with only two options that you had no say in. Looking deeper into the ballot is the best way to change who gets elected to Congress on a large scale. Vote in primaries. Engage on social media and with your friends and family. Do not just bandwagon with a front runner, find the best person for the job and make them the front runner.

Change does not happen overnight but by shifting voting margins, social media convos, donation trends, etc., we can create hard data that people are looking for something else. Once we start to show this, the money, media coverage, party support, and eventually winning elections will follow. We need Congresspersons who will put in the work required for the job, but we have to put in our shift first. Clock in now, because the shift is already underway.

4. Localize Local Issues and Nationalize National Issues

Increasingly, people are looking to smaller and smaller levels of government to address national level issues. And vice versa; looking for the federal government to make blanket rules and laws over nuanced or localized issues. It is important that we understand the different roles and capabilities of different governments within our federal system.

School board meetings in some communities are filled with folks who do not even have children in the school district fighting over culture war issues like race, gender, news media, and more. On the other side of the coin, the federal government has been expanding its power over time and is now a behemoth regulating everything you can think of under expansive interpretations of the commerce clause and other constitutional powers.

Our government was intentionally set up as a federal system wherein different levels of government have different powers. The state was intended to be the primary government in an average American's life. The constitution's bill of rights did not even apply to state governments until after the civil war, a process known as incorporation. States were free to restrict your free speech or quarter soldiers in your home. Only the federal government was restricted from doing so by the Bill of Rights in the United States Constitution.

Have you ever wondered why they used a constitutional amendment to criminalize alcohol but they simply pass laws (or delegate to an executive agency) in order to criminalize marijuana and cocaine and more drugs every year?

That is a prime example of expanding federal government power. When the 18th amendment was passed, the commerce clause was not interpreted as broadly as it is today. Constitutional issues surrounding the federal government's powers to police and regulate commerce that does not literally cross state lines or use navigable waterways were questionable at the very least. It was not clear that a regular federal statute would pass judicial muster. So amending the constitution proved to be the answer.

Today, the commerce clause gives the federal government extremely broad latitude in commerce of any sort. Besides goods literally crossing state lines, using routes of interstate commerce, and using implements of interstate commerce (such as internet or telephone), the commerce clause even allows the federal government to regulate wholly intrastate activity. I kid you not. If it is found to be part of a larger scheme to regulate interstate commerce, it is fair game.

To briefly summarize the 1942 case *Wickard v Filburn*, the supreme court ruled that it is constitutionally permissible for the federal government to enforce wheat production limits even on wheat that is grown and consumed entirely within one state. Their reasoning is that the intrastate activity affects the interstate market and thus could undermine the entire legislative scheme to regulate wheat. Consuming your own wheat means you do not have to buy it on the market, for example. This same reasoning was applied to the Controlled Substances Act regarding wholly intrastate marijuana in *Gonzales v. Raich*.

And voila, that's where the constitutional authority for federal drug laws comes from. This same sort of evolution has played out in numerous areas under several legal theories and covering myriad topics.

As the country has grown and the world has modernized, it does make some sense to centralize many areas of regulation. The commerce clause was largely intended to keep economic competition among states fair, after all. And now that we can buy anything from anywhere with the click of a button, it makes total sense for the federal government to regulate many aspects of commerce.

One way problems arise from these legitimate ideas, like regulating interstate commerce to ensure fairness, is when they are used as technical justifications for laws that are not about regulating commerce. Like federal laws criminalizing recreational drugs, for example. We all know that it is about the war on drugs as a social matter, not the economics of drug markets.

Not all of our problems need to be solved at the federal level. In fact, many types of laws and regulations work better at the state or local level. They allow for more nuance to apply to different populations with different conditions and different desires.

And likewise, it is neither wise nor necessary to bring federal issues to local venues. A lot of the driving force here is that people feel a lack of control over, say, federal immigration policy. They cannot rant to a session of Congress and demand action, but they can at the town hall or school board meeting. It can be a cathartic release, but ultimately detracts from the fundamental work the governmental units need to be doing.

Another driving force can be political theater, which will be further discussed later. But whatever the motivation is, this is a growing trend that needs to be reversed. If you will recall back to the discussions on Congress and the President, we want hard working, level-headed civil servants in those roles. The same applies to our local elections and we the people need to allow them to do their work.of course you can always lobby your representatives, that is what they are there for. But it is important to filter ourselves first and make sure that we are making an appropriate appeal in an appropriate venue. This ensures that our governmental resources (i.e. your tax dollars) are being used efficiently for the job for which they are intended.

As an aside to this section, I also want to quickly emphasize the importance of participating in local politics. At the very least, you need to take your vote in local elections seriously. Voter turnout soars in years with presidential elections, but there are other elections every year. Your one vote holds more individual power in your community than in a statewide or national election. The positions and issues on the ballot in non-presidential years probably impact your life more than you are aware... And in many cases, more than the president

5. Reduce Political Theater

This sort of thing was briefly mentioned in previous sections, but this goes beyond personality cults and Twitter trolls in Congress. The entire political arena is entirely consumed with political theater. From Speaker Pelosi ripping up President Trump's speech to the depths of Reddit and 4chan, one rule holds true: where there is politics, there is theater. In addition to refusing to support politicians who make their careers primarily on theater, personality, and slogans, we need to look closer to home for change.

Theater, to some extent, is inseparable from politics. Support must be gained, people must be persuaded. And it is generally easier and more effective to utilize snappy slogans and powerful visuals than to cogently lay out an entire political philosophy or nuanced position or legislation. This is obvious to anyone who has ever thought about it, but have we ever thought about challenging that norm?

For example, there was a spat in the House regarding a video in which Representative Paul Gosar's face was edited onto an anime character violently vanquishing his foes, including an edited-in Representative Alexandria Ocasio-Cortez. The video was posted on Representative Gosar's Twitter page and he was censured over it in a partisan vote. The argument in the House focused on whether it was a violent threat or political discourse.

Instead, I would question why this was evaluated by Representative Gosar and his team as something beneficial to post in the first place. Does it make him look strong? Committed? Effective? Relatable? You can judge for yourself if you have seen the video, but to my eye, it just looks silly and unprofessional. Why are memes more important than professionalism? Because voters have proven over and over that they respond to memes and other forms of theater more than they respond to professional responsibility.

And then I would question why House Democrats felt the need to make it official state business. I would be among the first to say how inappropriate the video is for a legislator to post. But I hate wasting state resources on further theater to counter his silly theater.

All this is something we can work to change, at least in our own little spheres. Normalize giving credit to politicians who stand for what is right, even if they are from another party. Skip news articles that talk about some outrageously theatrical act. Remind yourself that governance is a real job of serious business and not a television show or a sports team you root for or against.

Speaking of sports, remember when Vice President Mike Pence showed up at an NFL game and feigned outrage when players kneeled for the national anthem? He knew the players were going to kneel beforehand; it was happening at every game, every week. His secret service detail knew he was not going to stay for the start of the game. His motorcade was running and ready to go, having been told early in planning that Mr. Pence would not be in the stadium for long. The whole stunt was choreographed theater.

Various accountings of how much this stunt cost taxpayers come in around $325,000. You and I and our neighbors paid $325,000 for a publicity stunt, a traffic jam in Indianapolis, and subjecting tens of thousands at the game to the hassles of secret service security measures. All of this just for Mike Pence to throw his hands up and say how un-American it is to kneel during the anthem. A shameful display indeed.

Most acts of political theater do not literally cost us money. But there is an opportunity cost to us every time we engage with political theater. When we reward Representative Gosar for posting unprofessional videos or Democrats in Congress for regularly making censures state business by "liking," sharing, and engaging with content related to it, we are encouraging more of the same for the future. We are telling them, "spend your time and resources on this, not on the business of the country."

I have often wondered why symbols, stunts, and slogans have such a disproportionate effect on human behavior. When I see advertisements, my reaction is usually an eye roll and wondering to myself what sort of person would buy this thing based on this ad. And I think most people are the same. Internet users constantly complain about increased ads on YouTube videos and social media feeds.

Yet, all these terrible advertisements actually work. It's a numbers game. For all of us who roll our eyes, a handful of people take the ad to heart and will buy the product. I will even admit that when it comes down to two similar products, I'll go for the one whose name I recognize.... And usually that name recognition comes from advertisements.

Some people like the characters or catchy jingles and then ascribe other characteristics to the product that they could not possibly tell from the commercial. For example, people relate Progressive with being trustworthy and attentive because Flo, a longtime character from their television commercials, is portrayed as trustworthy and attentive. Obviously writing a character in that way does not actually say or prove anything about the company and their insurance products. But it works.

The same principles hold on political messaging and, of course, political theater. When I was younger, a big test for presidential candidates was who you "would like to have a beer with." This is a folksy way of saying that it is important for somebody to appear down to Earth and relatable. Presidents Bill Clinton, George W. Bush, and Barack Obama all excelled in this category.

But as history has unfolded, all three have been exposed as anything but relatable. Bill Clinton has a veritable encyclopedia of sexual indiscretions and a number of accusations that go beyond "indiscretion." George W. Bush is the son of a president and heir in a stupendously wealthy family (which we knew before, shame on us), as well as kind of a dunce with no spine (which we found out after). Barack Obama is now firmly entrenched with the political and Hollywood elite.

Marketing is an important part of capitalism and politics. You need to know what is out there in order to inform yourself. But the best way to view marketing and political theater is with a skeptical eye. You can take the claims to heart, but verify before acting (or voting). You can appreciate somebody's character, but do not put them on a pedestal. They are strangers, after all.

When you are aware that somebody is selling you something, you can evaluate the product in the proper context. Let's all be on notice and be aware that politicians engaging in theater are selling something to you. Act as you would when you are approached by a guy with a bad tie on a car lot.

6. End Tribalism

Surprised it took so long to get here? We need to dig out of our entrenched identity positions in order to move our country forward. I intentionally use the term identity instead of partisan or ideological because this issue is more complex than that. More than at any time since the Vietnam era, Americans are making their politics a core part of their identity. And they are also making their identity a central part of their politics.

Identity politics has become a term of art used by people with certain criticisms about wokeness, etc. That is a part of this discussion, but it goes much deeper and much broader than that. Consider the discourse around the hardcore supporters of Donald Trump. Years after his election loss, there are still Trump 2020 signs and flags displayed all over conservative leaning parts of the country. His diction style, his terms and phrases, his Twitter peculiarities, everything he said and did became something for his supporters to emulate . They buy everything with his name on it and proudly display their support of him every day of their lives on their home, on their vehicle, and on their person.

To Trump supporters, this level of dedication is proof of how much he is adored. To others, it is evidence of a cult. To anybody with an objective eye, an unusual number of Trump supporters have adopted this man and his politics as a core part of their identity. It is an interesting phenomenon that may be the loudest and most notable example of a growing trend in all corners of modern American politics.

Consider the grassroots internet support and the infamous Bernie Bros supporting Senator Bernie Sanders when he ran for president in 2016. The devotion of his most intense supporters was not entirely dissimilar from the phenomenon we see around Trump. The numbers and the demographics were significantly different, but the underlying emotional attachment appears similar.

Both were framed as outsiders fighting an unfair system. Both were claimed to have the parties and the political elite working against them. Both drew national media attention on some of the bad sides of their most intense supporters, like internet trolling and violence at events. Both of them made it easy for people who felt overlooked to grab on to their message and take it to heart. Both were the subject of memes and rhetoric framing them as saviors and warriors and game changers.

And, arguably, it is the very passion of their most fervent supporters that ended up costing them elections. Bernie Sanders supporters became associated with the most radical of leftist ideals and that perception cost him electability points in the minds of primary voters and the DNC. Likewise, when all of the loud, obnoxious assholes yelling at immigrants, punching flight attendants over masks, and saying racist things online were obsessed with MAGA and other Trumpisms, it made it very easy to rally broad support against Donald Trump.

When we make politics, and especially politicians, a core part of our identity, it obstructs exchanging ideas, compromise, and working together. It feeds the toxic rhetoric that pervades political spaces and obstructs progress.

Virtues like freedom and equality are very important and it does make emotional sense to make them a part of you. Passion is a powerful tool and is what fuels real social and political change. But it is necessary to keep certain boundaries in place in order to maintain intellectual integrity and avoid being taken for a ride.

First of all, you do not need to be an expert, an activist, or even have an opinion on every issue. Or even on every case within the scope of your issue. For example, a trend in the realm of criminal justice reform is to highlight certain cases of perceived inequality or unfair treatment. Oftentimes, the actual issues being highlighted are lost in a version of the telephone game on social media. And also often, the cases being highlighted are framed in a misleading manner to appear a greater injustice than they were.

Consider this publicized case from 2021: There was a man in prison for shooting and killing somebody during a robbery. It then came out that there may have been a member of the jury who harbored a racial bias against the defendant's race. There were calls for the man to be given a new trial with a new jury. But by the time the issue reaches some of the idiots and influencers of social media, it becomes "free this man and drop all charges," which is objectively insane. Based on the evidence, it is most likely that this person did commit the murder in question. It is insane to give a murderer a free pass because a 1/12 of a jury was alleged to be racist. Taking strong stances like this without understanding the issues and facts undermines the whole movement, provides fodder for opposition, and has potential to derail progress.

And that is just one case of criminal justice reform. Multiply that by a few thousand, add vaccines, economics, and everything else that people spout off about with a passion that far exceeds their knowledge. All this to say that you do not need to advocate for every prisoner, pretend to be a medical researcher with every vaccine, or be a Google lawyer for every law. You do not need to stake a passionate position on everything. Gather the facts and make sober decisions and judgements.

As the saying goes, never meet your heroes. The implication being that they are built up with a certain unassailable public image and rarely live up to it. This is doubly true with politicians. But instead of not meeting them, you should not let them be heroes or influential over you to that degree in the first place.

They are not superheroes. There is no savior coming. These are men and women trying to get hired for a job. They have flaws in their character and their abilities. They might have some altruistic intent, but every one of them has some selfish motivation too.

Whether career, money, power, legacy, or something else, there is something that they want out of it.

Identifying too closely with a politician or leader clouds your judgment with them and prevents you from accepting criticism of them. It is important to keep them at arm's length. They are professionals you hire, not friends or family.

"Professionals you hire" gets to the core of the issue here. You need to evaluate them as you would evaluate a contractor for your home or a lawyer for your divorce. Do the flashy commercials actually do anything for you? Are they putting in the hours necessary? Do you actually like the outcomes or do you just like the person?

As far as identity politics go, that is a street that runs both ways. It is most often used to describe perceived wokeism or simply voting for minorities for diversity's sake. But it reaches other realms too. Christianity is perhaps the most influential identity in politics even to this day. Every president has been a Christian, at least nominally in public. A large majority of Congress are Christians even though polls show that the United States is the least religious it has ever been.

Representation is important because there are some issues that are best addressed by those who lived them, among other reasons. But representation is also a marketing technique, a part of political theater. Consider the selection of a presidential candidate's running mate. Joe Biden selected Kamala Harris because she is a woman of color. Donald Trump selected Mike Pence because he is a rust belt evangelical. Pure identity politics on both accounts.

We cannot allow identity to replace substance. Identity is best accounted for as a contextual complement to the underlying substantive evaluation of a candidate. Identity for identity's own sake inevitably leads to tokenism. And bear in mind that ideology and party affiliation can be the sort of identity this is based on; it is not just race, ethnic, sex, and gender. There are places all over the country where identifying as R or D makes all the difference. A Republican is not going to become mayor of New York City for the foreseeable future and a Democrat is not going to be the governor of Nebraska based entirely on that one identifying characteristic which, let's be real, describes more than just how a candidate intends to vote.

7. Figure Out Money

Money in politics mucks the whole thing up. Who do politicians really work for? Are they acting out of duty or self-interest? Is it fair for them to both regulate and invest? What is the real reason behind any act of government or candidacy?

These are legitimate questions for the public to ask. But when they get asked in government circles, things get hushed up real quick. Before discussing what needs to be done on this front, we first need to come to at least somewhat of an understanding of what the heck is even going on.

The term "lobbying" is frequently misused in contemporary discourse to refer narrowly to shady dealings, usually involving money, between politicians and big money special interest groups and corporations. This is a demonstration of ignorance. Lobbying includes anything anybody does to inform, persuade, pressure, or encourage the government to act in a certain way. Sending an email to your Congressional Representative's office is lobbying. Holding a sign outside a government building is lobbying. Lobbying is an integral part of representative democracy. Nobody can represent you if you do not tell them what you want them to do.

So let's try to narrow down this complex topic to what exactly we are talking about and why we take issue. To start, let us consider the most fundamental operational question about campaigns: How should they be funded?

There is some support for a structure where campaigns are funded by the government. This would allegedly level the playing field and keep money from unsavory sources out of American politics. I reject this solution outright for a number of reasons.

This method still keeps unresolved many of the primary questions raised by cases like Citizen's United and even complicates them further. What is to be done about advertisements, documentaries, even social media posts by people unaffiliated with the campaign? If we restrict it, that is a significant restriction on political speech, the antithesis of free speech. If we do not restrict it, what is the point of the state funding official campaigns? Money they would otherwise raise could simply be redirected to "unaffiliated" groups.

There are some intriguing ideas for hybrid solutions out there. One example is small donor public finan-cing, a system in which public funds match and multiply small, individual dona-tions. New York City has a match and multiply system in which a $50 dona-tion gener-ates a total of $350 for the candid-ate. Proponents say it has helped reduce the influ-ence of special interests and empower aver-age voters. Small donor public finan-cing aims to incentivize candid-ates to seek out many individual support-ers instead of just a few big donors. Because it does- not restrict polit-ical spend-ing, it may stand up to the Supreme Court's require-ments from Citizen's United and subsequent cases. But it may also raise new legal issues in the coming decades.

Other approaches to public campaign finan-cing include voucher systems, where citizens receive certain amounts in public funds they can direct to their preferred candid-ates. Tax cred-its for small campaign dona-tions are another way to encour-age more people to parti-cip-ate and to allow candidates to fund their campaigns without relying on corporations and super PACs.

Self-funding remains as a viable option. This does seem to favor special interests and the wealthy. But I will again ask you to adjust your perspective. We have the numbers and thus the power to influence these things. We are not beholden to them. You do not have to allow television ads to buy your vote. You can research who is paying for what. Social media is an incredible tool for activism and there are groups who track campaign donations and expenditures, travel of politicians and the ultra-wealthy, and more. Knowledge and money are both weapons in the political realm. We can use knowledge to counter money. Rather than restricting huge swathes of money and speech, let us simply require transparency and we can do the leg work ourselves.

If campaigns are funded by oneself or money one raises, that prompts a next obvious question: How do we keep campaign money and personal money separate?

The nuances here are intriguing. Allowing campaign contributions to a candidate from a normal person makes all the sense in the world. But people are less comfortable when that average individual is replaced with a special interest group or corporation or billionaire.

We can all mostly agree that even if campaign contributions are ok, literally paying somebody personally to vote a certain way or adopt a certain position is not. I think most people at least suspect that there are under the table exchanges that go along with political campaigns. Perhaps they are tied to above board campaign contributions in most cases, perhaps not.

To be totally frank, all of this is just to highlight how complicated the issue is and how difficult it is to make fair, enforceable rules. It is vitally important to target corruption where we can, but it is a practical fact that it is not easy to find, prove, and prosecute.

What we can do to fill in the gaps is to use public records and internet sleuths to crowdsource this information. I mentioned earlier about people tracking the ultra wealthy, etc. This sort of thing combined with campaign fundraising records and public statements about positions and votes can be used to build a circumstantial case pointing to corruption. The ballot box is not a court of law and nobody has a fundamental right to hold an elected position. We do not need proof beyond a reasonable doubt to merely choose to vote somebody else. We simply need to act pragmatically and reach the best conclusion for the good of our community.

Transparency and dissemination of information can be more effective than money in influencing political discourse. As long as we are willing to vote out those who breach our trust, we can effectuate this change through voting rather than drowning the whole system in red tape.

Part 2

With these principles in mind, I would like to discuss some policy
positions that may serve as productive starting points to viable,
reasonable solutions. This is not a strict platform, merely a
discussion of policy.

Guns

Gun ownership is an individually protected right under the Second
Amendment. But it has traditionally been treated as a lesser right by
the courts. In instances of judicial review, fundamental constitutional
rights are typically treated with strict scrutiny. Strict scrutiny means
that in order for a law or government action to be allowed to infringe
on such a right, it must be narrowly tailored to achieve a compelling
government interest.

Strict scrutiny is generally applied to fundamental rights like in First
Amendment cases and Fourteenth Amendment racial discrimination
challenges. Second Amendment cases are not treated so favorably.
They do not even use a consistent standard between federal circuits
or even between different cases oftentimes.

With the Supreme Court affirming that individual gun ownership is a
right granted by the plain language of the constitution, it is time to
stop treating it as a second class right. Courts need to begin treating
Second Amendment challenges like they treat free speech and
racial discrimination. It needs to be reviewed under strict scrutiny.
This would make it as strong of a right as its inclusion in the Bill of
Rights would indicate.

But recall that standard of strict scrutiny. Narrowly tailored to
achieve a compelling government interest. Even the *Heller* Supreme
Court decision recognizing gun ownership as a protected right
acknowledges that long-standing, reasonable gun restrictions are
constitutionally sound.

The thing gun restriction laws will always have working for them is that it will always be about saving lives, at least in the government's legal position. It is much, much easier to argue that saving lives from gun violence is a compelling government interest than any sort of speech restriction or racial bias.

Recognizing the nature of gun ownership rights will not mean that those rights are unlimited. What it will do is protect the fundamental right of gun ownership while allowing the courts to build consistent jurisprudence under a consistent standard. What sorts of gun restrictions are allowed and what are not will be whittled down over time, as with free speech cases, once we have a clear structure and appellate courts can confidently take up these cases with clear guidance.

A basic goal of government regulation is to maximize public safety while minimizing costs to individual liberty. One way to do that is by tailoring rules to places or situations where they're likely to do the most good.

The biggest differences on gun views are between urban people and rural people. And it makes perfect sense. They have different experiences with guns, different lifestyles, and different reasons for supporting or restricting guns. I would suggest that in a constitutional review, such differences should factor in. New York City banning pistols in taxis is more compelling than Tawas, Michigan doing the same.

Consider the following thought experiment: If there are 100 people in an urban area and 40 in a surrounding rural area voting on a gun restriction referendum together, let's say 80 urban and 6 rural will vote in favor of it. When it passes, 86 people are happy, and 54 people are unhappy. If they each vote on referendums for their own local area, it will pass in the city and fail in the country, 114 people (80 urban and 34 rural) will be happy, and 26 people (20 urban and 6 rural) will be unhappy.

It is a bit crude, but demonstrates how allowing more local control can lead to more people satisfied with outcomes. Of course what this does not address, and is a huge obstacle, is the fact that gun markets, traveling, and criminal networks are all things that occur on a national scale. I recognize the problems that patchwork laws can cause in this regard. For example, it may allow somebody to simply travel to a neighboring jurisdiction to get around their own location's gun laws. Or an otherwise law abiding citizen has to carefully plan his route and research dozens of laws to travel with his firearm.

I envision this localized framework to be more effective on possession, ownership, concealment, and use than on purchasing. I do believe that states and the federal government can put together a solid framework that includes reasonable precautions with guns which do not trample Second Amendment rights. But I do not believe that I have any novel ideas on this front. There are tons of proposed solutions out there. From universal background checks to a federal database to banning certain weapons and so on. When evaluating these ideas, we first need to ask whether they are constitutionally sound. Let's apply our ideal standard of strict scrutiny and look for solutions that are narrowly tailored to achieve a compelling government interest. How can we allow the most freedom for keeping and bearing arms while still achieving our goals?

This is where we throw out "ban all guns," "SHALL NOT BE INFRINGED," and other entrenched, unconstitutional, partisan positions. This is where we seek utility and effect, fairness and reasonableness. I do not know which particular idea or combination of ideas would be the best. But I do know that there is a solution out there that will protect all of these competing interests. We need to be willing to engage and evolve in order to find it.

Voting

Joe Biden won the 2020 election. There was no major voter fraud, there was no communist conspiracy. The people pushing those claims are dishonest, partisan hacks. There were not huge lists of dead voters, Venezuela and China did not hack election machines, and January 6 was a disgusting display of overt political violence, for which Donald Trump is largely responsible.

If you disagree with any of that, you're just an idiot. This book is not for you.

The push by the political right to use these absurd lies as casus belli to restrict voting and empower partisan officials to take over elections is extraordinarily alarming. There are racial components to this, certainly partisan components, and the whole thing is dishonest and authoritarian.

The political left is often disingenuous about voting too. Voter ID requirements are not inherently racist and there are reasons besides naked discrimination that felons cannot vote, for example. This is another case where we have to put partisanship aside and evaluate what is honestly reasonable and what is not.

Requiring some form of voter identification is reasonable. Cherry picking the sorts of acceptable IDs to discriminate against people is not. Let's allow for ID requirements, but accept many forms of ID or provide IDs for free in a hassle free way, like through a simple online ordering process.

Mail in voting is reasonable. There is no reason to suspect there is significant fraud through mailed ballots. Hours long lines that happen to frequently occur in black, urban areas are unreasonable. Commit the necessary resources to allow people to vote without taking a day off work.

Day off work, that's an idea. Why are elections held on Tuesdays? Back in the early days of our democracy, there were fewer polling stations and travel was more difficult. Tuesday allowed people to attend church on Sunday, travel to the capital or county seat on Monday, vote and travel back home Tuesday, and be back Wednesday for the farmer's market. I kid you not, this is the historical reason.

Since none of those concerns are all that concerning in our modern times, it basically comes down to "because that's the tradition." If it was a Saturday or Sunday, it would allow more people to vote without interfering with work. If it was a national holiday, it would affect work, but many more people could vote easily. It seems silly to have so many holidays to celebrate everything from presidents to labor rights to religion, but we cannot have a single day for this most vital civic practice

Beyond the laws and rules and regulations, we need to examine our own behavior around elections. Alarmist election rhetoric and propaganda was completely out of control in 2020. 2024 is shaping up to be worse and 2016 wasn't so great either. This is a distressing trend. Part of the problem simply lies in understanding the facts.

Some Democrats did not really understand the "election interference" discussions in 2016 and thought that Russia literally hacked voting machines. This is asinine. Many Republicans thought foreign communists used Italian satellites to hack voting machines in 2020... Among many, many wacky, stupid conspiracy theories. All of these things are easily disproved and one simply needs to look into the basic facts with a rational eye.

Of course the granddaddy of all of these conspiracies is the racist claims that Barack Obama was not born in America. Even before that though, the alarmist reactions were clearly going to push things in that direction. I remember people crying when Bill Clinton defeated Bob Dole. I remember claims that George W. Bush was going to destroy the country. I remember claims that Barack Obama was going to destroy the country.

Spoiler alert: The country has not been destroyed. No matter who is elected president, somebody is going to throw a fit about it. But rather than continually relitigating past elections, we will turn our energy to the next issue, the next election, the next step. We will not react emotionally, but logically.

Policing

Two things can be true at the same time. For instance, police officers often have a very hard job, but police officers are also generally not held to a very high standard for all of the authority and trust we place in them. Police officers are often asked to put themselves in dangerous situations, but police officers often make situations dangerous.

I would like to share a couple of anecdotes from my rebellious youth. One time when I was leaving a college party with my brother and a friend, my drunk brother decided to step off the side of a parking lot and urinate in a wooded area. A police officer apparently pulled in, saw him back there, and stopped to investigate. My brother yelled, "Run!" My friend and I, who had kept walking and were not aware of what was happening behind us, started to jog as we turned around. We saw the officer, stopped jogging, and laughed at my brother's luck. We continued walking on our way and joking around.

A minute or two later, two squad cars come screaming around a turn in front of us, spotlights on us and everything. 4 cops jump out and next thing we know, we are all lit up with laser sights. "Don't fucking move!"

A bit excessive, don't you think? This is the sort of overly aggressive, militarized policing that makes everything look like a nail for a cop to hammer.

Here is another. I was working overnights at McDonald's in college and was driving home at 4:30 AM. I was pulled over for having an expired registration tag. The problem? My tag was not expired and in fact was only a month old. I told the officer this, I showed the registration, I told him that it says the month and year right on the damn sticker... And yet, I didn't get anywhere. He insisted it was the wrong color. It was not. Meanwhile while I argue with Officer Dumbass, his partner slinks- literally slinks, looking like the Pink

Panther cartoon- to the slightly cracked open passenger window. I watch the whole thing in my mirror and peripheral vision. He walks all shady and sneaky up to my window and sharply inhales. He was trying to smell pot. They saw a long haired kid at 4:30 AM in a college town and decided to fabricate a reason to pull him over to look for weed. They ended up "letting me go" with a "warning."

Folks, I'm white and I get harassed by the police like this. As a criminal defense attorney, I can tell you that my situation is not unique. People, and especially people of color, have legitimate grievances on this topic.

Speaking of my lawyering career, this is the difference between becoming a police officer and becoming an attorney. In the time it took me to get my undergraduate degree, my law degree, take the bar exam, and get licensed, a guy I knew did the following:

He was a year younger than me, so he spent that first year finishing high school. Then he went to a community college program to become a preacher or something along those lines, I am not sure the exact title. He did that for a bit and decided he didn't like it. So he went back to community college, this time in a policing program. He finished his schooling and did his law enforcement certifications. He finished that, got a job, and worked as a sheriff's deputy for over a year before I got my law license.

Lawyering is a serious vocation with serious responsibilities, it makes sense that there is so much that goes into it. But my goodness, I do not carry a firearm. I do not chase people in vehicles or physically handle them. I cannot write a ticket or charge anybody with a crime. Police education and training focuses too much on training the firearms and tasers and hand-to-hand self-defense and restraining techniques and driving techniques and not enough on protecting rights or even application of the law.

I would like to see higher standards for police. There are some novel ideas out there about how to take some burdens off of police and shift them to specialists who are specially trained and equipped for certain situations. We can separate mental health response, traffic accident documentation, medical response, even traffic enforcement from the people responding to and investigating serious violent crime.

Like other areas of government, we need to treat different localities differently. Police in violent gang areas should be trained and equipped to deal with that. Police who normally kick teens out of a small town park should not be armed with high-powered weapons and have a utility belt to rival Batman. We need to use the right tools for the right jobs.

Another quick point is that I would encourage you all to support good policing. Yes, continue to call out bad policing. But policing is a difficult job and if we thank and recognize those who do it well, it can help create a culture where officers strive for that sort of thing, people trust the officers in their communities, and we can change the whole national attitude around policing.

Immigration

Part of what makes immigration such a complicated issue is that it is explicitly (per the constitution) an area of law designated to the federal government. But immigration and borders shape society and culture completely in some areas of the country and hardly at all in others.

Consider the different experiences and how the people have their views shaped in a Texas border town vs an immigrant neighborhood in New York vs rural New Hampshire. Unfortunately, immigration is not something that can be localized. It requires a single policy set at the federal level.

On that note, a quick aside on so-called sanctuary cities. While I personally disapprove of actions by municipal actors that appear to actively thwart immigration enforcement, I stand firm on constitutional grounds that the federal government cannot compel or coerce other governments to do its job for it. This is known as anti-commandeering. Immigration is the federal government's job and they cannot commandeer state or city governments to enforce immigration in its stead. We must hold to this principle consistently or else this will be another area, like the commerce clause and executive power, where federal power expanded to the point where we have to denounce it in wordy manifestos like this.

With that in mind, let's return to operative immigration policy. If immigration enforcement is conducted under a cost/benefit analysis with some deference to the places most affected by it, that lays a groundwork where all Americans can be confident in the efficient use of their tax money as regards immigration while allowing local communities and border states can have a say in matters that most affect them directly.

Choosing where to spend immigration enforcement resources should be aimed more at criminal or tax avoiding people than "low hanging fruit" who pay taxes and are known in the community. This is not a moral judgment, merely a calculated one. It costs money to detain somebody, house them while you initiate proceedings, facilitate court, and follow through with deportation. If that money is going to be spent, it is more efficient to spend it on clear economic and social "takers" rather than economic and social "givers."

But it is also important to defer to some degree to smaller units of government and society when appropriate. Some communities benefit more than others from immigration and some communities are burdened. When the federal government is responsible for immigration enforcement and is told by a community that they are being burdened by illegal immigration, the feds need to take that seriously. Enforcement can be shaded toward those communities that feel burdened and away from communities that feel bolstered. The feds still have the final say of course, but the key word here is cooperation. The different units of government need to work together for workable solutions.

As far as securing the border, physically constructed barriers are not the way. We can cover way more ground and act much more effectively with electronic surveillance and manpower. Drones, cameras, and sensors can alert agents to the locations of border crossers. And perhaps more importantly, they can create a detailed digital record of who crossed where and when. This allows resources to be targeted at proven routes as they change on a weekly or monthly basis.

We can also make our borders more secure and efficient with some creative ways to get more bang for the buck. The borders could provide excellent live action training opportunities for reconnaissance, surveillance, and security. I am talking about military, national guard, law enforcement, perhaps even private industry. K9 handlers in border regions can regularly be trained at border checkpoints. Military police, reconnaissance units, drone pilots, the possibilities are too numerous to list. This would allow our budget to be used more effectively.

Military Budget

The United States spends huge sums of money on the military beyond every other country in the world. On the one hand, it is important to project American power globally in order to secure some degree of order in a chaotic world and to protect American interests where necessary. But on the other hand, the Department of Defense is objectively bloated with bad, inefficient spending and continuously locked into bad contracts for failing or unneeded equipment. When you have such a big hammer, everything looks like a nail and we need to take to heart the lessons taught by modern armed conflict.

First, let's address ideology. We are seeing a swell in isolationist tendencies among Americans, no doubt in part because of the budgetary, political, and humanitarian quagmires in Iraq and Afghanistan. Russia is now experiencing the same thing in Ukraine. No matter where in the world or who is fighting, it has become clear that even advanced modern militaries simply cannot take and hold large areas of land by force. Weapons are too disseminated, people are too interconnected, populations are too large, and too many other actors are sticking their fingers in.

So isolationism makes sense... At least to the extent that we do not need to invade and occupy every place in the world where trouble pops up. However, it is still important, and perhaps more so than ever, to maintain a strong presence in many strategically important parts of the globe. If we do not keep up the pressure in the South China Sea, China will eventually expel by force every other country from the area and control global shipping. It was the United States Navy that mostly cleared out pirates from the Gulf of Aden in the last decade or so. It's easy to say "let somebody else do it," but then how do we know it is going to get done? High achievers take care of business and the United States is a high achiever.

One direction we can move in to make our global presence more efficient is to close down redundant military installations overseas and keep fewer troops and less equipment constantly overseas. There are over 35,000 US military personnel stationed in Germany alone at a cost of a little over $8 billion in 2020. At least several thousand of them could come home without risking security in Europe. Japan and South Korea are filled to the brim with US military bases and together host some 80,000 personnel, for which we spend over $11 billion. The numbers are staggering. Relatively small cuts could save huge amounts of money in total.

Bad contracts are another reason why military spending is so notoriously inefficient. The Department of Defense enters into huge, long term contracts for development and production of complex new weapon systems. Let's use a tank to serve as an example. This is a new tank with all the bells and whistles. Ablative armor, anti-projectile defenses, digital aiming systems. But 2 years in and it's behind schedule, having battery problems, and this type of projectile defense has become obsolete.

The way things work now, the military has to ride out or pay off that contract. The reasons for why these contracts are so huge and long are numerous, including political interests (military-industrial complex), the economics of developing cutting edge technology, and the time it takes to see a huge project through. But enough is enough. The military cannot be bogged down by contracts and politics.

The Department of Defense needs to require that contracts longer than 2 years feature a no penalty opt out clause. To balance the economic interests, we can require that the military has to give good faith first consideration to the same company in how to spend the money saved by breaking the contract. But if a contractor cannot deliver a cutting edge product or come up with another idea, they do not deserve corporate welfare. Wasting taxpayer dollars merely to sustain some jobs is peak inefficiency. That money can be spent in a way that creates jobs AND benefits the country.

LGBT Rights

One legal element that should be applied more broadly is that all LGBT discrimination is sex discrimination. We do not need a whole new class of protected characteristics, we need to apply already existing protections to people who are being discriminated against.

Imagine somebody does not a get a job because he is a homosexual man. Stated another way, he did not get the job because he is a man who is romantically interested in men. Would this company also refuse to hire a woman who is romantically interested in men? No? That's discrimination based on sex. The only difference between those scenarios is the sex of the applicant. This is covered under existing discrimination laws, it only needs to be properly applied as such.

But the hot topics on LGBT issues these days largely center around which spaces trans individuals should occupy, from bathrooms to sports teams and more. These issues raise some interesting questions around fairness and social divisions. Much of how we feel about these things comes down to how we view the goals and reasons for separated spaces in the first place.

For example, those who view sports as a serious competitive endeavor with life changing opportunities tend to favor excluding trans women from women's sports. People who view sports as mere recreation, exercise, and socializing tend to favor allowing trans women to compete in women's sports. We should be able to recognize that sports are all of those things. There is a lot on the line at higher levels of sport. Money, scholarships, prestige. But for a majority of people, sports are never going to be anything more than a good time and a conduit for life lessons.

Life lessons are an important consideration because they are always discussed around youth sports. Sports teach teamwork, responsibility, and so on. Trans youths need to learn those things too. Title IX, the federal law addressing sex discrimination in education, impacts sports by the reasoning that scholastic sports are a part of education, including in colleges and universities. This reasoning is exactly why it is important to include everybody in sports regardless of their biological and social categorization.

On the other hand, Title IX has been interpreted to require equal funding for athletic scholarships in men's and women's sports. When trans women are being awarded women's scholarships, it certainly raises some questions about Title IX. Without debating what constitutes a woman, it is without question that at least the spirit and intent of this aspect of Title IX is being violated if "people born with penises and testicles" have 51% of scholarships and "people born with vaginas and ovaries" have 49%.

The accounting question will remain up for debate. To address competition, I believe there is a relatively simple solution for high level sports: You have a division for cis women, females, sex assigned female at birth, etc. And you have an open division. It's not for men, it's purely based on merit. Anyone only needs to be good enough to make a team. This would withstand judicial scrutiny due to application of intermediate scrutiny recognizing the inherent biological differences between most people born with female genitals and most people born with male genitals. Trans individuals do not experience the same differences to the same degrees and thus would compete in the open division.

And lower levels of sport, I only hope for a set up where everyone is allowed to play. College scholarships, records, Olympics are one thing. But let's make sure that every child has a spot on a team somewhere.

Education

Higher education needs to be provided by the government. This is not for the benefit of individuals, who will certainly benefit as well, but for the very survival of the country in a global economic marketplace. It is no secret that Americans are being beaten by much of Asia and Europe in all areas of academics, most notably science and math.

I would push back on the notion that people might waste "free" degrees on "useless subjects" with a question: So what? Let them go get another degree if that's the case. China selects people for certain jobs or paths and trains them for that purpose. They have over a billion people to choose from. The one advantage we have is freedom. If everybody is able to get do-overs and end up in a position where they can be more productive, everybody wins. The economy, the individual, and the state.

One must consider that cost being a primary barrier to higher education removes a huge number of people from the candidate pool. Among the huge numbers of a country with over 330 million people, it is highly likely that many highly competent individuals are being screened out by their family's financial situation.

And on the other side, high costs mean that many students who may not be as competent feel pressured to go into a field that they feel will justify the cost of the education. It is an economic analysis of cost/benefit and forward looking job markets by a teenager. It's absurd. No wonder average students feel the need to pursue advanced engineering degrees and otherwise brilliant students are convinced by a rep from the philosophy department that employers love philosophy majors. People are not finding the right fields to thrive in because it is all about money.

By the way, this all includes training for trades and such too. The government should pay for it all. The more options people have, the more efficient they will be over the course of their working life, even if it takes a few extra years to become settled. Someone who has failed out of college should not be too scared or too poor to then go to trade school because of the debt hanging over him. Society benefits most if he becomes a skilled welder or something instead of setting into whatever job will pay his bills at the moment.

If the whole point of education or job training is to sacrifice now for a pay off later, why is it naturally assumed that this risk falls on the individual? The state has a stake in this too and is in a much better position to absorb the risk. When an individual pays for his own education, it is all or nothing in some ways. When the state does so, it is spread out over many different investments. Any financial advisor or gambler will tell you that this is the safest way to earn a consistent return. You hedge your bet and spread your risk. This state funded education virtually guarantees that everyone is allowed and encouraged to fulfill their potential, which benefits the entire country.

Of course education does not begin after high school. In order to secure our place in the global pecking order, we need to do a better job of educating our young people. Schools are often focused too much on essentially crowd control and babysitting and too little on high quality education. The most gifted students often do not feel challenged. Huge portions of students fall behind merely because of lacking effort.

While there are certainly changes to be made in policy, I would like to focus on what we can do first. Our culture does not broadly value knowledge. It does not value education as anything other than job training. Before expecting schools and governments to finish the job, we need to start changing attitudes in our homes and communities.

What do you think when I say that our culture does not value knowledge? Perhaps it clashes with what you feel like you see and experience. But what could be mistaken for valuing knowledge is actually about being taken in by charisma and sales tactics.

My mother, bless her heart. She is an older woman who lived most of her life before the technology we take for granted. She was convinced that Best Buy's Geek Squad were computer experts who are there to fix computers. I had to explain to her that they are 19 year old salespeople who will ALWAYS try to get her to buy another Best Buy product.

Raise your hand if you've heard this before: "Donald Trump is the best person to fix tax loopholes since he knows all of them." Do you think he files his own taxes on TurboTax? No? He pays accountants and tax attorneys? So why don't we elect the tax attorneys then? Remember the "the nuclear is very powerful" speech? The "Barron is very good with the cyber" thing? We clearly value charisma over knowledge... Or at least do not know how to recognize one from the other.

And what about education? Everybody wants their kids to go to college, that's valuing education, right? The problem is two-fold: There are some who outright ignore or hold disdain for education and there are some who nominally value education, but only with lip service or in a narrow context of job training.

I find that disdain for education is often cultural and ideological, while ignoring it is often rooted in the practical and challenges life presents. Anti-intellectualism is a real and growing trend in our country. But even more broadly than that, the ideas of truth and objectivity are under constant assault. It is more important than ever to teach intellectual skills to children with the same gusto as we teach them values or religion or chores.

Many Americans feel that they do not understand what their children are learning in school or do not have time to help with education on top of work and other obligations. This is especially true in single parent households and households where both parents work full time.

This is why it is important to cultivate community education. By pooling our intellectual resources, we can create more engagement with education. If you cannot help with your child's homework, do you know somebody who can? Are there other students who live nearby? Even getting older kids to tutor is a great way to teach patience, responsibility, and community to the older kids while also helping the younger kids academically.

On a policy level, standardized tests encourage a narrow view of education and results in teachers teaching the test material rather than a well rounded education. Rather than certain facts on certain subjects, the quality of education should be evaluated based on skills. Reading comprehension and writing are good foundations for children because they are skills that can be applied broadly and can be tested fairly easily. Critical thinking and other skills can be added, while narrow memorization based tests should be phased out.

Incarceration

I am confident that a recital of United States incarceration statistics is not necessary for us to agree that prisons are a problem in this country. The rates at which people are committing real crimes is certainly a large part of this equation, but I wish to zero in on incarceration here. Prisons do play a part in crime rates due to networking, culture, and lack of rehabilitation, among other factors. More effective prisons would lower rates of recidivism.

The first thing we need to do is not incarcerate so many damn people. Jail and prison should not be a time out; it should serve the logical uses of all of those iron bars and concrete walls: to keep the community safe from dangerous criminals.

Some people sit in jail for months waiting for trials over simple drug possession cases. People who fudge numbers on a loan application or violate probation get locked up with violent criminals. Incarceration has become too automatic, too expected in our society. Whenever I see a news story on the internet covering a criminal sentencing, I always know what the most popular comments are going to be: "ONLY x years/months?!?!" This is often followed by a suggestion for several decades in prison and people calling for the judge to be "fired."

I get it, crimes can evoke passionate responses. But does 8 months or 1 year or 8 years or 20 years in prison even mean anything to the average person? It's virtually meaningless, people are just saying numbers.

Rather than treating incarceration like adult time out, it should be used to keep dangerous criminals away from the public. No non-violent criminal should spend substantial time behind literal bars. We need to shift our focus to what is best for society rather than a base desire for retribution.

A thief cannot repay what they stole if they spend years in prison and have difficulty finding work. Perhaps they should be put on a payment plan and retrained for certain kinds of work that do not have access to money or expensive equipment. It is all about efficiency and maximizing positive outcomes for society. I know many want to see criminals locked up for punishment's own sake, but that only drains resources. Drug possession should either be decriminalized or treated as a minor infraction with an emphasis on rehabilitation. Keeping drug users in the work force and around family and friends is the best economic and social outcome. Prosecution and incarceration only burdens everyone further, including taxpayers.

Citizens in 45 states vote for their top prosecutor, usually at a county or city level. A study found the number of trials increased nearly 10 percent during election years with an incumbent running for reelection. When there was a challenger, the number rose an additional 14.7 percent. Generally speaking, cases that go to trial are sentenced more harshly than those that plea. So it is literally true that prosecutors send more people to prison for longer when they are running in a contested election.

The content of prosecutor campaigns does nothing to encourage effective, responsible job performance. They emphasize the quantity of cases won at trial rather than qualitative measures of conduct or the decision making framework that reflects how the prosecutor approaches the job. Low public interest and uncompetitive elections stack the deck heavily in favor of incumbents and anyone with name recognition, regardless of their prosecuting chops. Once in office, the pressures of reelection make too many prosecutors agents of mass incarceration.

Judges feel many of these same pressures. There is significant statistical evidence showing that judges facing election challenges are more likely to deliver harsh sentences, less likely to overturn death penalties, are more likely to be especially harsh on black defendants, and that all of these trends increase as election day nears.

It is practically a universal rule that people are more likely to hear about and react to an overly lenient sentence than an overly harsh one. The worst thing for an elected criminal court judge to be labeled in the electorate is "soft on crime." In a district where these elections line up, a defendant may be dealing with a prosecutor and a judge who both benefit politically and professionally by giving him a harsher sentence.

Ultimately, we have to recognize that locking up criminals is not a measure of how effectively our criminal law systems work. A judge who gives harsh sentences is not necessarily a good judge, a prosecutor who seeks maximum sentences is not necessarily a good prosecutor, and a society is not necessarily deterring crime when it locks up huge portions of its population.

Conclusion

By applying some of the principles discussed here, we can reverse the trends of our toxic, self-serving political sphere. An ideological tug of war is a perpetual stalemate like two tugboats pulling opposite ways. But a rising tide raises all ships and that is exactly what responsible, constitution based governance is all about: raising the tide to leave all the muck behind.

The most important thing any of us can do to encourage competent government is to vote. And not just in presidential elections. Protect school boards from insane conspiracy theorists. Make sure the judges in your community are ethical. Vote in drain commissioners and city council members who take the job seriously. No political ax grinders, no wannabe professional politicians. Competent professionals to do a professional job.

We can do this. Thank you for reading and God bless America. I'll see you out there.